SPACE SCIENCE

Planets

By Simon Pierce

Published in 2024 by Cavendish Square Publishing, LLC
2544 Clinton Street Buffalo, NY 14224

Copyright © 2024 by Cavendish Square Publishing, LLC

First Edition

No part of this publication may be reproduced, stored in a retrieval system, or transmitted in any form or by any means—electronic, mechanical, photocopying, recording, or otherwise—without the prior permission of the copyright owner. Request for permission should be addressed to Permissions, Cavendish Square Publishing, 2544 Clinton Street Buffalo, NY 14224. Tel (877) 980-4450; fax (877) 980-4454.

Website: cavendishsq.com

This publication represents the opinions and views of the author based on their personal experience, knowledge, and research. The information in this book serves as a general guide only. The author and publisher have used their best efforts in preparing this book and disclaim liability rising directly or indirectly from the use and application of this book.

All websites were available and accurate when this book was sent to press.

Library of Congress Cataloging-in-Publication Data

Names: Pierce, Simon, author.
Title: Planets / Simon Pierce.
Description: Buffalo, NY : Cavendish Square Publishing, [2024] | Series: The inside guide: space science | Includes bibliographical references and index.
Identifiers: LCCN 2023029766 | ISBN 9781502670199 (library binding) | ISBN 9781502670182 (paperback) | ISBN 9781502670205 (ebook)
Subjects: LCSH: Planets–Juvenile literature. | Solar system–Juvenile literature.
Classification: LCC QB602 .P488 2024 | DDC 523.4–dc23/eng/20230815
LC record available at https://lccn.loc.gov/2023029766

Editor: Jennifer Lombardo
Copyeditor: Jill Keppeler
Designer: Deanna Lepovich

The photographs in this book are used by permission and through the courtesy of: Cover Anterovium/Shutterstock.com; p. 4 Mr.Kuiku/Shutterstock.com; p. 6 Bertini fresco of Galileo Galilei and Doge of Venice/Wikimedia Commons; p. 8 NASA/JHUAPL/SwRI; p. 9 Meletios Verras/Shutterstock.com; pp. 10, 16 Juliasuena/Shutterstock.com; p. 12 (main) PlanilAstro/Shutterstock.com; p. 12 (inset) NASA/Johns Hopkins University Applied Physics Laboratory/Carnegie Institution of Washington; p. 13 NASA/Nicole Mann; p. 15 NASA/JPL-Caltech/ASU/MSSS; p. 18 NASA/JPL-Caltech/SwRI/MSSS; p. 19 NASA, ESA, A. Simon (GSFC), M.H. Wong (University of California, Berkeley) and the OPAL Team; p. 21 (main) Lawrence Sromovsky, University of Wisconsin-Madison/W.W. Keck Observatory; p. 21 (inset) NASA/JPL; p. 22 NASA; p. 24 Jurik Peter/Shutterstock.com; p. 25 BEST-BACKGROUNDS/Shutterstock.com; p. 27 doomu/Shutterstock.com; p. 28 (top) frantic00/Shutterstock.com; p. 28 (bottom) Don Pablo/Shutterstock.com; p. 29 (top) D1min/Shutterstock.com; p. 29 (bottom) sdecoret/Shutterstock.com.

Some of the images in this book illustrate individuals who are models. The depictions do not imply actual situations or events.

CPSIA compliance information: Batch #CWCSQ24: For further information contact Cavendish Square Publishing LLC at 1-877-980-4450.

Printed in the United States of America

CONTENTS

Chapter One: 5
   Finding the Planets

Chapter Two: 11
   The Inner Solar System

Chapter Three: 17
   The Outer Solar System

Chapter Four: 23
   Exoplanets

Think About It!   28

Glossary   30

Find Out More   31

Index   32

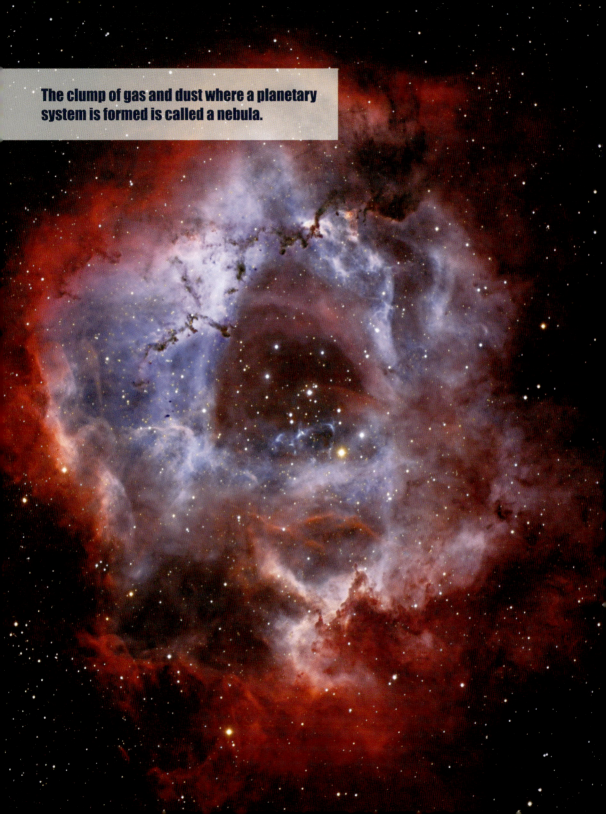

The clump of gas and dust where a planetary system is formed is called a nebula.

FINDING THE PLANETS

Chapter One

About 4.6 billion years ago, a cloud of gas and dust came together in space to form our sun. The leftover material formed clumps that became the planets, asteroids, comets, and everything else in the solar system. The sun's gravity pulled everything into orbit around it.

Finding the Planets

From Earth, people can see five planets without a telescope: Mercury, Venus, Mars, Jupiter, and Saturn. Early civilizations tracked the movements of these planets, along with the stars. They used this information for things such as trying to **predict** the future and figuring out the best times to plant and harvest crops.

After the telescope was invented in 1608, **astronomers** were able to see the planets in more detail. They also realized that there were more planets in the solar system than people had thought. However, they didn't have a clear idea of what a planet was. In fact, even today, astronomers are still learning about the planets and what they are.

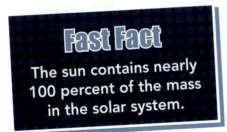

Fast Fact
The sun contains nearly 100 percent of the mass in the solar system.

Early telescopes weren't very powerful, but they were better than the naked eye.

CLASSIFYING CERES

Ceres is an object in space that has been **reclassified** several times since its discovery. At first, astronomers believed it was a planet. It was first seen in 1801, before Neptune was discovered, so Ceres became the eighth planet. In 1851, astronomers decided it was too small to be a planet, so they called it an asteroid instead.

In 2006, when the formal **definition** of a planet was created, astronomers reclassified Ceres again. As of today, it's the only **dwarf** planet in the inner solar system. Ceres is the largest object in the asteroid belt, but it's much smaller than Earth's moon.

Finding All the Planets

By 1846, astronomers had found 13 objects they called planets. However, by 1851, they had reclassified some of the smaller planets as asteroids, leaving the solar system with only eight planets. In 1902, an astronomer named Percival Lowell started to think there might be a ninth planet beyond Neptune. He couldn't see this planet, but he noticed something strange about the orbits of some comets. He believed the way they moved in a certain part of space showed that they were moving around a planet.

Fast Fact

The word "planet" comes from the Greek words *asters planetai*, or "wandering stars." The Greeks noticed that some stars—which we know today are planets—moved differently than other stars.

An object named Charon orbits Pluto. Some people say Charon is Pluto's moon. Others say it's another dwarf planet because it's so big.

Up until his death in 1916, Lowell kept trying to prove that this planet, which he called Planet X, existed. Other astronomers finally found the planet, which they named Pluto, in 1930.

What Is a Planet?

In 2006, a group of astronomers decided that they needed a formal definition of a planet. The definition they came up with says that a space object is only a planet if it orbits the sun, has enough mass to pull itself into a round shape, and has enough gravity to force objects that are about the same size out of the way of its orbit. Pluto didn't fit this last part of the definition, so it was reclassified as a dwarf planet.

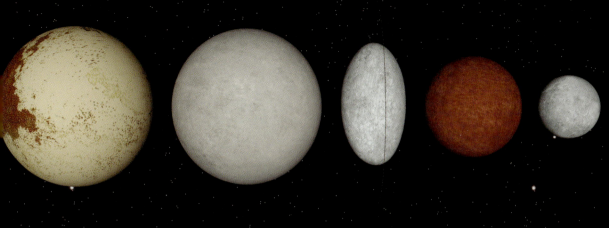

Pluto　　Eris　　Haumea　　Makemake　　Ceres

This picture shows some of the best-known dwarf planets in our solar system.

Fast Fact
There are two ways a planet can clear things out of its orbit. It can push them off into space, or it can pull them into its own orbit.

Right away, some astronomers didn't like the new definition. In 2021, a group of astronomers said the definition of a planet should be anything in space that's geologically active. This means its surface changes on its own over time. However, others argued that this isn't a good definition, either, because it includes too many objects. If geological activity were the only thing an object needed to become a planet, our solar system would have more than 150 planets—possibly including our own moon! Astronomers are still trying to decide on the best definition.

This picture shows the planets that make up the inner solar system.

THE INNER SOLAR SYSTEM

Chapter Two

Our solar system is divided into two parts: the inner solar system and the outer solar system. An asteroid belt is the dividing line between them. Earth is part of the inner solar system, along with Mercury, Venus, and Mars. "Inner" and "outer" are directions relative to the sun, which is the center of the solar system.

Mercury

Mercury is the closest planet to the sun. It's also the smallest planet—only a little bigger than Earth's moon. Like all the planets in the inner solar system, Mercury is a rocky planet. It has solid ground but no **atmosphere**. This makes it very hot during the day and very cold at night.

Mercury rotates more slowly than Earth does, so one day on Mercury is the same as 59 days on Earth. However, since it's closer to the sun, it takes less time to complete one orbit. For this reason, one Mercury year is equal to only 88 Earth days.

Fast Fact
Mercury and Venus are the only two planets in the solar system with no moons at all.

Venus

Since Mercury is the closest planet to the sun, it seems reasonable to believe this would also make it

11

These lines on Mercury were formed when an object hit the planet and threw dirt and rock in all directions.

the hottest. However, the hottest planet in the solar system is Venus. This is because Venus has a thick atmosphere that traps heat, much like a greenhouse does on Earth.

In 2012, people watched Venus pass between Earth and the sun. This picture shows how small Venus is compared to the sun.

Venus

Scientists believe that more than 1 billion years ago, Venus might have been covered in oceans that could have held life. However, all the water boiled away, leaving a dry, rocky surface. Spacecraft sent to Venus have been destroyed by the heat and pressure of the atmosphere.

Earth

Our home planet is the only one in the solar system that can support life. Many different things had to be a certain way at the same time to allow life to grow. For example, our atmosphere is thick enough to hold the sun's warmth in, but not so thick that we overheat or are crushed.

Earth also has a magnetic field around it because there's iron in the planet's core, or center. This magnetic field stops **particles** from

Astronauts often take pictures of Earth. This picture from 2023 shows a tropical storm called a cyclone forming over the country of Mauritius in the Indian Ocean.

THE ASTEROID BELT

The asteroid belt is made up of millions of leftover pieces from the solar system's creation. It lies between Mars and Jupiter and stretches across 140 million miles (225 million kilometers). Most of the asteroids in the belt are very small. Three of them are more than 250 miles (400 km) across.

By studying asteroids, scientists have learned that these space bodies have a lot of metals in them, such as gold and iron, that could be used on Earth. However, mining an asteroid in space would be hard and dangerous, or unsafe, so no one has tried it yet.

the sun, called solar wind, from blowing the atmosphere away.

Mars

Mars is often called the "Red Planet" because it has a red glow in the sky. Thanks to scientists who sent vehicles called rovers to Mars, we know why it's red. The dirt on Mars, which scientists call regolith, has a lot of iron in it. When iron meets oxygen, it rusts.

Fast Fact

Once in a while, the sun gives off a stream of particles called a solar flare. These particles reach Earth's upper atmosphere, where **satellites** orbit the planet. The solar flare's energy doesn't hurt people, but it can make the satellites stop working for a little bit.

For many years, people believed aliens lived on Mars. Today, even though we know it isn't true, people still like to think about what it would be like if Martians were real. Scientists are studying Mars to see if there was life there billions of years ago, when the planet was warm enough to have liquid water on its surface.

Fast Fact

One day on Mars is less than an hour longer than one day on Earth. However, because Mars is farther from the sun, its year is nearly twice as long as an Earth year.

Scientists think these curved bands of rock on Mars were created by a fast-moving river billions of years ago.

This picture shows the planets that make up the outer solar system.

THE OUTER SOLAR SYSTEM

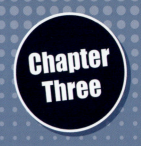
Chapter Three

Jupiter, Saturn, Uranus, and Neptune are in the outer solar system, past the asteroid belt. Beyond Neptune is an area of space called the Kuiper Belt. Like the asteroid belt, the objects that make up the Kuiper Belt were left over from the creation of the solar system.

Jupiter

The planets in the outer solar system are known as giants. This is because they're much larger than the inner solar system planets. Jupiter and Saturn are called gas giants because they have little or no solid ground. Jupiter is the largest of all the planets; in fact, all the other planets could fit inside it!

Jupiter has cold winds that blow the gases of its atmosphere across the planet. Seen from space, these look like bands of color. It also has a swirling red spot near the **equator** on one side of the planet.

Fast Fact
Jupiter has about 95 moons. Until 2023, that was the most of any planet in the solar system. However, scientists recently discovered 62 new moons around Saturn, bringing its total to 145.

Fast Fact

Seasons happen when a planet is tilted toward or away from the sun. All the planets in the solar system have seasons, but the others' weather is very different than Earth's. Venus is hardly tilted at all, so it has the least difference in its seasons.

These swirls near Jupiter's north pole are storms. They're smaller than the red spot, but they're still miles wide.

This is a storm larger than Earth that has been going on for hundreds of years.

Saturn

Saturn's **iconic** rings make it instantly recognizable. In pictures, the rings look solid, but that's only because they're spinning so fast. They're made up of billions of small pieces of ice and rock. Scientists believe these rings were made from pieces of rocky space objects that were torn apart and pulled in by Saturn's gravity when they got too close to the planet.

The Hubble Space Telescope took this picture of Saturn in 2019.

Saturn's atmosphere has too much heat and pressure for anything to live there. However, some of its moons might be able to support life. For example, the moon Titan is covered in ice, but scientists believe it has liquid water underneath that ice.

Uranus

Uranus is known as an ice giant because its atmosphere is made up of icy gases. The planet does have a rocky core. Although the gases are icy, they hold heat in, which makes Uranus about 9,000 degrees Fahrenheit (4,982 degrees Celsius) at its center!

Like Saturn, Uranus has rings, but they're much harder to see. What makes Uranus **unique** among the planets is that it rotates on its side.

THE EDGE OF THE SOLAR SYSTEM

The Kuiper Belt marks the end of the planets in our solar system. The belt is a doughnut-shaped band of icy space rocks, including Pluto. The Kuiper Belt is very big, cold, and dark. Scientists know very little about it because it's so hard to see from Earth. It would take about 10 years to travel there from Earth.

Far past the Kuiper Belt is another large area of icy, rocky bodies known as the Oort Cloud. It's sometimes called the edge of the solar system because this is where the sun's gravity stops pulling things toward it. It's even harder to see than the Kuiper Belt. It would take 300 years just to get there, and up to 30,000 years to get past it.

Scientists don't know exactly why this is. One idea is that an Earth-sized object crashed into Uranus billions of years ago and knocked it sideways.

Neptune

Neptune is another ice giant. It's so far from the sun that it hardly gets any light. This makes it hard to see, even with a telescope. Scientists used math to figure out that it was there. Most of the time, Neptune is closer to the sun than the dwarf planet Pluto. However, every 248 Earth years, Pluto moves closer to the sun than Neptune for a 20-year period.

> **Fast Fact**
> Methane gas makes up a large part of Neptune. When methane is crushed under a lot of pressure, it turns into diamonds. For this reason, it likely rains diamonds deep within Neptune!

This picture shows Uranus from both sides. Because its rings are visible, it's easy to see its sideways tilt.

Neptune is tilted at about the same angle as Earth. However, because it takes so long to complete one orbit around the sun, each of its seasons lasts for 40 years!

Neptune's deep blue color comes from the methane in its atmosphere. It absorbs, or soaks up, red light and only reflects, or bounces back, blue light.

Each of the dots in this picture is a galaxy, and each galaxy holds trillions of planets.

EXOPLANETS

Chapter Four

Planets outside our solar system are known as exoplanets. Scientists didn't find any until 1992, but since then, they've found thousands. More are being found all the time. On March 25, 2022, the National Aeronautics and Space Administration (NASA) **confirmed** its 5,000th exoplanet. As of 2023, the count is up to about 5,500.

What We Know

For a long time, scientists thought exoplanets probably existed, but they couldn't prove it. Space is too big, stars are too bright, and planets are too dim. Telescopes weren't powerful enough to see them. Even with the improved **technology** we have today, it's still hard to find exoplanets. The fact that scientists have already found so many shows just how many are out there!

Fast Fact
Some exoplanets orbit two stars at once. Others don't orbit any star at all.

Direct imaging is one way scientists find exoplanets. This is when a telescope looks right at the planet. Deep space telescopes such as the Hubble Space Telescope and James Webb Telescope have made direct imaging easier. However, since the planets are still very

23

far away from the telescopes, they show up only as points of light. We don't know what they look like on the surface, although scientists can sometimes guess based on things such as the color of the light the planet gives off.

Fast Fact

Once, scientists thought the most common kind of exoplanet was what they called a "hot Jupiter." Hot Jupiters got their name because they're about the size of Jupiter and very close to their star. However, they later realized hot Jupiters aren't very common, they're just the easiest to find from Earth.

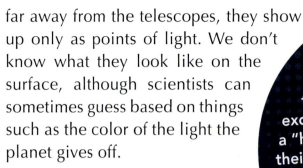

This picture is one artist's idea of what an exoplanet might look like.

Scientists built the James Webb Telescope to take pictures of places in space we can't get to with today's spaceship technology.

Most exoplanets are too small or too close to their star to see through direct imaging. Scientists use math and science to figure out where these planets are. For example, when a planet passes in front of its star, scientists can measure the amount of light it blocks. This tells them how big the planet is and what its orbit is like.

A CLOSER LOOK AT EXOPLANETS

There are many kinds of exoplanets. Some are bigger than Jupiter and hot enough to rain liquid metal. Others are the size of Earth, but so far from their star that they're covered in miles of ice. A handful seem to be similar enough to Earth to possibly support life, but scientists don't know that for sure right now.

One of the most Earthlike exoplanets we know of is called Kepler-452b. It's 60 percent larger than Earth, and its star is 10 percent larger than our sun. The planet's year is only 20 days longer than an Earth year. Another Earthlike planet is TRAPPIST-1e, which scientists think could have more water on it than there is in Earth's oceans.

What We Don't Know

Many astronomers would be very excited to find another planet like Earth, especially if it already has life on it. Life might exist in a very different form than we're used to on planets that aren't like Earth, but humans would never be able to visit them to find out. If scientists find another very Earthlike planet, humans could travel or even live there.

Fast Fact

Someday, billions of years from now, Earth won't be a good place to live anymore because the sun will reach the end of its life. Many people like the idea of having another Earthlike planet to move to before this happens.

Scientists still don't know how many planets are out there, whether any of them hold life, or whether humans could visit them. They might never know because of how long it would take to get there. With the technology we have today, it would take more than 6,000 years just to get to Proxima Centauri b, the closest known exoplanet to Earth. For now, all we can do is keep studying exoplanets from a distance.

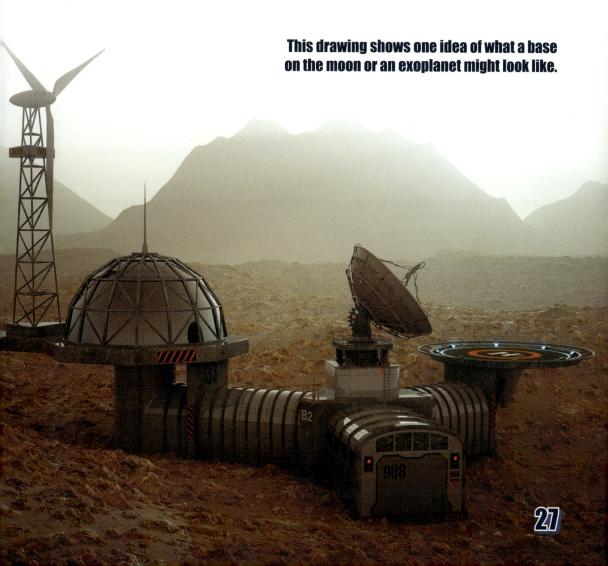

This drawing shows one idea of what a base on the moon or an exoplanet might look like.

THINK ABOUT IT!

1. How would the world be different if the telescope had never been invented?

2. What makes Earth different from the other planets?

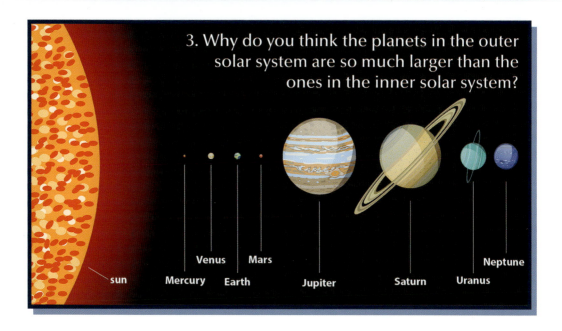

3. Why do you think the planets in the outer solar system are so much larger than the ones in the inner solar system?

sun   Mercury   Venus   Earth   Mars   Jupiter   Saturn   Uranus   Neptune

4. Do you think humans will ever live on another planet?

GLOSSARY

astronomer: A scientist who studies space.

atmosphere: The mixture of gases that surrounds a planet.

confirm: To find to be true.

definition: The meaning of a word.

dwarf: Of less than the usual size.

equator: The imaginary line around the middle of a round object, such as a planet.

iconic: Widely recognized and well-established.

particle: A very small piece of something.

predict: To guess what will happen in the future.

reclassify: To move from one category to another.

satellite: A man-made object or vehicle intended to orbit the earth, the moon, or another heavenly body.

technology: A method of using science to solve problems as well as the tools used to solve those problems.

unique: Special or the only one of its kind.

FIND OUT MORE

Books
Rose, Rachel. *Planets*. Minneapolis, MN: Bearport Publishing, 2021.

Stott, Carol. *Planets*. New York, NY: DK Publishing, 2023.

Thacher, Meg. *Sky Gazing: A Guide to the Moon, Sun, Planets, Stars, Eclipses, Constellations*. North Adams, MA: Storey Publishing, 2020.

Websites

BrainPOP: Solar System
www.brainpop.com/science/space/solarsystem
Watch a movie, play games, and take a quiz to test your knowledge of the planets.

NASA SpacePlace
spaceplace.nasa.gov/all-about-exoplanets/en
Read more about how scientists find exoplanets.

National Geographic Kids: Passport to Space
kids.nationalgeographic.com/space
Learn more cool facts, and take a look at some amazing pictures of our solar system.

Publisher's note to educators and parents: Our editors have carefully reviewed these websites to ensure that they are suitable for students. Many websites change frequently, however, and we cannot guarantee that a site's future contents will continue to meet our high standards of quality and educational value. Be advised that students should be closely supervised whenever they access the internet.

INDEX

A
asteroids, 5, 7, 14
asteroid belt, 7, 11, 14, 17

C
Ceres, 7, 9
Charon, 8
comets, 5

D
dwarf planets, 7, 8, 9

E
Earth, 5, 7, 11, 12, 13, 14, 15, 18, 20, 21, 24, 26
Eris, 9
exoplanets, 23, 24, 25, 26, 27

G
gravity, 5, 8, 18, 20

H
Haumea, 9

J
Jupiter, 5, 14, 17, 24, 26

K
Kepler-452b, 26
Kuiper Belt, 17, 19

L
Lowell, Percival, 7, 8

M
Makemake, 9
Mars, 5, 11, 14, 15
Mercury, 5, 11, 12
moons, 7, 8, 9, 11, 17, 19, 27

N
NASA, 23
nebula, 4
Neptune, 7, 17, 20, 21

O
Oort Cloud, 20

P
Pluto, 8, 9, 20
Proxima Centauri b, 27

S
Saturn, 5, 17, 18, 19
sun, 5, 8, 11, 12, 14, 15, 18, 21, 26

T
telescopes, 5, 6, 20, 23, 24, 25
Titan, 19
TRAPPIST-1e, 26

U
Uranus, 17, 19, 20, 21

V
Venus, 5, 11, 12, 13, 18